WHO AM I?

I am big and bulky, grey and wrinkly.
I live in Africa.

WHO AM I?

By Moira Butterfield
Illustrated by Wayne Ford

Belitha Press

First Published in the UK in 1996 by
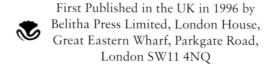
Belitha Press Limited, London House,
Great Eastern Wharf, Parkgate Road,
London SW11 4NQ

ISBN 1 85561 572 X

British Library in Cataloguing in Publication Data for this book
is available from the British Library.

Printed in Portugal

Editor: Jilly MacLeod
Designer: Helen James
Illustrator: Wayne Ford / Wildlife Art Agency
Consultant: Andrew Branson

My ears are large.
I've got big feet.
I use my trunk to drink and eat.
My skin is wrinkly,
tough and grey.
I take a muddy bath each day.

Who am I?

Here is my trunk

I use my trunk to pull leaves and twigs from the trees and put them in my mouth. I eat nearly all day long.

Every day I bathe in the river. I use my trunk to drink the water. Sometimes I spray water on to my skin.

Here are my tusks

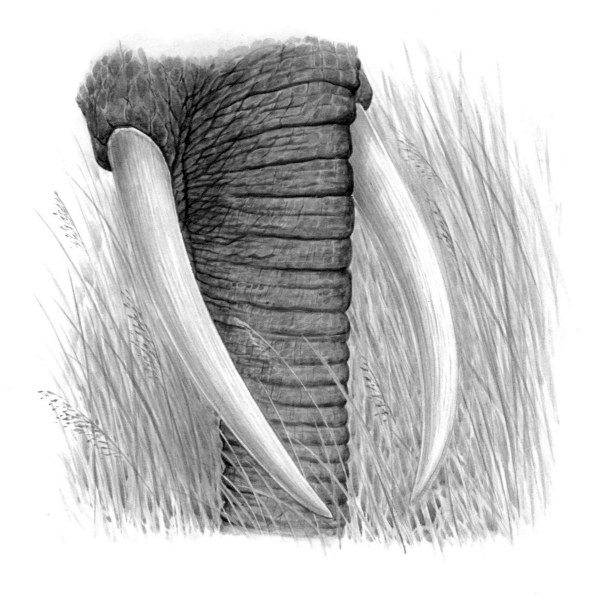

I have two tusks that stick out from my mouth. They are long and sharp. I use my tusks to tear up grass to eat.

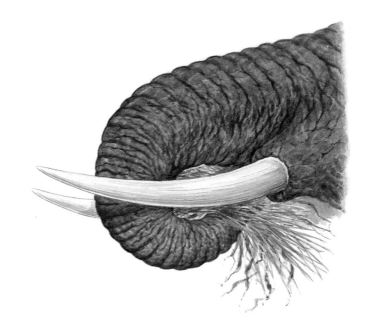

If something makes me angry, I charge at it with my tusks sticking out. Look how fast that lion is running away.

Here is my ear

I flap my big ears to keep myself cool. The place where I live is always very hot in the daytime.

When the sun feels too hot, I stand under some shady trees. How many birds can you spot in the branches?

Here is my tail

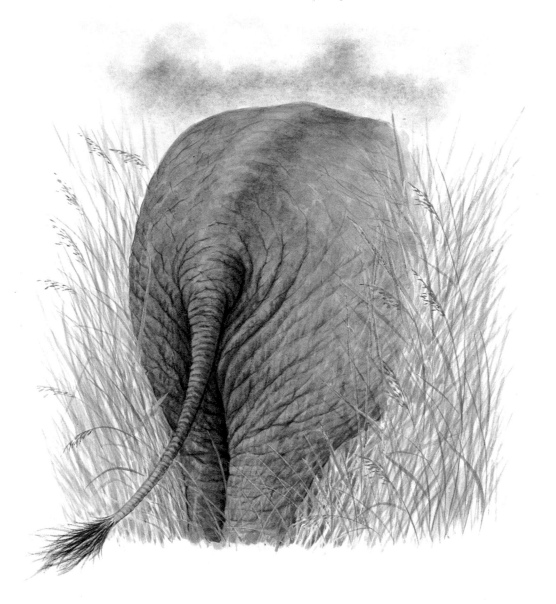

I swish it to keep away the flies that buzz around me all day long. There are lots of flies where I live.

Sometimes an egret bird sits on my back and pecks at the flies. I do not mind giving the egret a ride.

Here is my skin

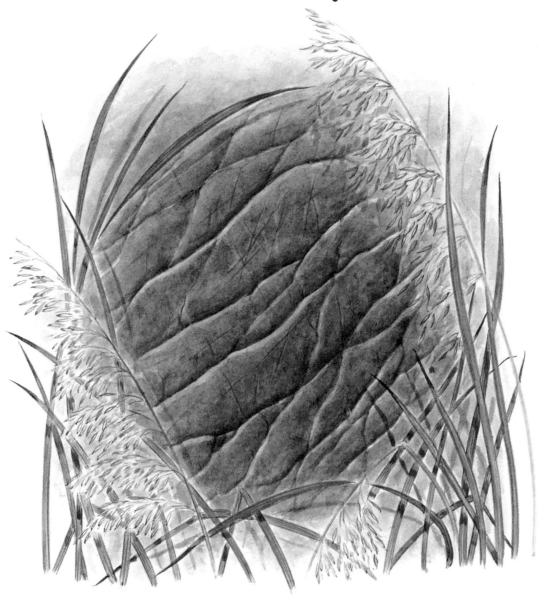

It is grey and wrinkly and is about three centimetres thick. I like to sprinkle dust on it to keep it soft.

I love to roll in slippery sloppy mud. When I get up, the mud dries on me and helps to keep me cool.

Here is my foot

My feet are as round and wide as tree trunks. My whole body is very, very big and heavy.

I can run and swim and stand on my back feet to reach up high. Sometimes, I even sleep standing up.

Here is my eye

If I see something that frightens me or makes me angry, I warn my friends by making a loud noise.

I lift up my trunk and...
trumpet!
Have you guessed who I am?

I am an elephant

Point to my...

big ears

long trunk

wrinkly skin

four feet

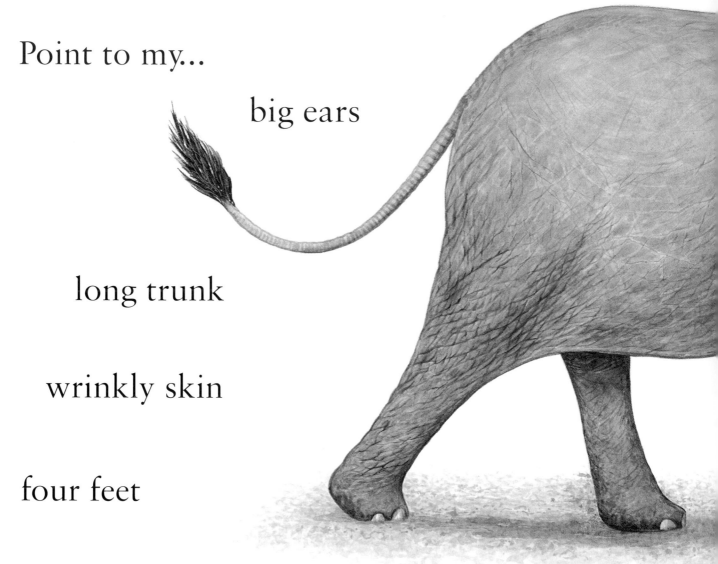

sharp tusks

swishing tail

I am called
an African
elephant

Here is my baby

She is called a calf.
I am her mother
and I look after her.
We live with some
other elephants in
a herd.

Sometimes my calf
plays with the other
baby elephants.
They love to splash
about in the river.

Here is my home

I live in grasslands.

Can you see me with my herd?
How many zebras, lions, giraffes
and antelope can you find?

Here is a map of the world

I live in a hot land called Africa. Where is it on the map?

Can you point to the place where you live?

Africa

Can you answer these questions about me?

What do I use my trunk for?

What do I like to eat?

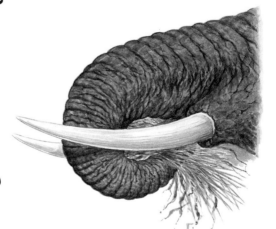

Where do I bathe every day?

What noise do I make when I am angry or frightened?

Why does the egret bird sit on my back?

What is my baby called?

What colour is my skin?

Is my skin smooth like yours?

What do I do with my ears
to keep myself cool?

Here are some words to learn about me

calf The name for one of my babies.

grasslands The large grassy plains where I live with the rest of my herd.

herd The family of elephants I live with.

skin The thick grey covering over my body. You have skin too. What is yours like?

shady A cool place where there are shadows. I stand in a shady place when I want to keep out of the hot sun.

sloppy Something that is runny and watery, like the messy wet mud I like to roll in.

trumpet The loud noise I make when I am scared or angry. Can you make a trumpeting noise too?

trunk My long nose. I use it when I am eating and drinking.

tusks The long pointed teeth that stick out from my mouth.

wrinkly Something that has lots of creases and folds in it, just like my skin.